# Lakes

## Catherine Chambers

Heinemann Library

© 2000 Reed Educational & Professional Publishing
Published by Heinemann Library,
an imprint of Reed Educational & Professional Publishing,
Chicago, Illinois

Customer Service 888-454-2279

Visit our website at www.heinemannlibrary.com

Designed by David Oakley
Illustrations by Tokay Interactive
Originated by Dot Gradations
Printed in Hong Kong/China

06 05 04 03
10 9 8 7 6 5 4 3 2

**Library of Congress Cataloging-in-Publication Data**
Chambers, Catherine, 1954-
    Lakes / Catherine Chambers.
        p. cm. – (Mapping earthforms)
    Includes bibliographical references (p. ) and index.
    Summary: Explores the world's lakes, discussing how they were formed, what organisms live there, and how they are used by humans.
    ISBN 1-57572-524-X (lib. bdg.)        ISBN 1-4034-0034-2 (pbk. bdg.)
    1. Lakes—Juvenile literature. [1. Lakes.] I. Title.
GB1603.8.C48 2000
508.16'9221—dc21
                                99-043374

**Acknowledgments**
The Publishers would like to thank the following for permission to reproduce photographs: Still Pictures/Paul Harrison, p. 4; Aspect Picture Library Ltd./T. Okuda, p. 5; Still Pictures/R. Seitres, p. 7; Robert Harding Picture Library, p. 8; Oxford Scientific Films/B. Littlehales, p. 9; Still Pictures/J. Wark, p. 10; Oxford Scientific Films/S. Osolinski, p. 12; Corbis, p. 14; Still Pictures/E. Cleigne, p. 15; Oxford Scientific Films/C. Milkins, p. 16; Bruce Coleman Limited/B. and C. Calhoun, p. 17; Bruce Coleman Limited/Dr. M. Kahl, p. 18; Bruce Coleman Limited/R. Meier, p. 19; Robert Harding Picture Library/R. Francis, p. 20; Oxford Scientific Films, p. 24; Panos Pictures/H. Bradman, p. 25; Ecoscene/S. Donachie, p. 26; Still Pictures/H. Schwarzbach, p. 23; Still Pictures/Eastlight, p. 29.

Cover photograph reproduced with permission of Robert MacKinlay and Still Pictures.

Some words are shown in bold, **like this.** You can find out what they mean by looking in the glossary.

# Contents

# What Is a Lake?

A lake is a large body of water that is surrounded by land. Lake waters can be either fresh or salty. Some lakes are found high in the mountains. Other lakes are at sea level or below. All lakes are fed by rain, springs, streams, or rivers. The water in lakes is never completely still. We will see how the earth's **water cycle** affects the lakes of the world.

Lake Titicaca is the largest lake in South America, and at 12,500 feet (3,811 meters) above sea level, the highest **navigable** lake in the world. Years ago, Incans lived on its shores and on islands in the middle.

## How have lakes formed?

Lakes have formed in many different ways. Some have been formed by **glaciers scouring** out hollows in the earth's surface. Other lakes occur in dips at the bottoms of folds in masses of rock. Still others form in the craters of **extinct** volcanoes. Lakes are also formed when **landslides** block valleys. Some lakes fill huge cracks, or **faults,** that are made when the earth's crust moves. Others are formed where rivers cross flat valley floors. Still more are formed when people build **dams.**

## What do lakes look like?

Lakes can be very small. Many small lakes are found high in the mountains or low on river **flood plains**. Other lakes, called ribbon lakes, are long and thin. Many ribbon lakes lie in huge cracks in the earth's crust. Other lakes are vast inland seas. We will see how lakes fill different shapes and how man-made lakes have altered the landscape. We will also find out how lakes change over time.

## Life in and around lakes

Many freshwater lakes have a lot of plant and animal life. But some lakes have very little life in and around them. Some saltwater lakes teem with fish, but in very salty lakes, there is little visible life. Plants and animals that live in or near lakes have **adapted** to the lake environment. We will see why some lakes attract living things and what the future holds for the lakes of the world.

 Lake Biwa, Japan's biggest lake, is an important waterway connected to the Kamogawa **Canal**. It provides power to the city of Kyoto. Lake Biwa is a beautiful lake. It is a sacred lake for the Japanese people. Many poems have been written about it, and it is featured in Japanese legends.

5

# The Lakes of the World

Lakes are everywhere in the world. They range in size from huge lakes, called seas, to small lakes on islands. Lakes can lie in cool, wet areas, or in hot, dry areas. Lakes are found in high, rocky mountains, on **plateaus**, and on low, flat **plains**.

Lakes can fill **basins** in the wet parts of the year and then disappear in hot, dry weather. Some lakes disappear completely over time, and some new lakes form.

 This map shows the world's ten largest lakes. You can see that lakes occur in hot, dry areas, as well as in cool, wet areas. In desert areas, such as the Sahara, there are huge underground lakes.

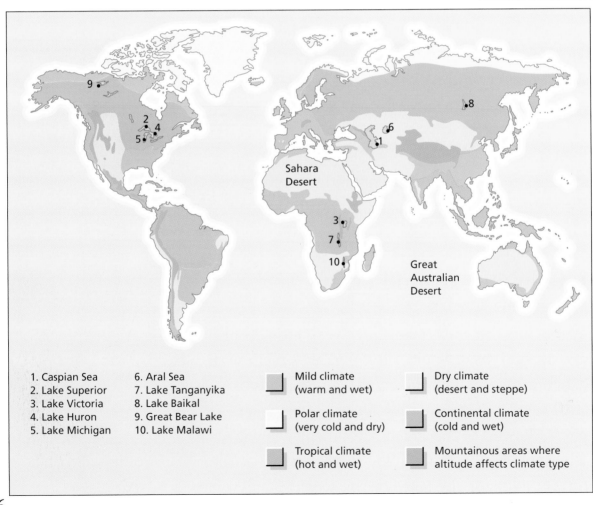

Sahara Desert

Great Australian Desert

| | |
|---|---|
| 1. Caspian Sea | 6. Aral Sea |
| 2. Lake Superior | 7. Lake Tanganyika |
| 3. Lake Victoria | 8. Lake Baikal |
| 4. Lake Huron | 9. Great Bear Lake |
| 5. Lake Michigan | 10. Lake Malawi |

Mild climate (warm and wet)

Polar climate (very cold and dry)

Tropical climate (hot and wet)

Dry climate (desert and steppe)

Continental climate (cold and wet)

Mountainous areas where altitude affects climate type

## Big lakes and small lakes

Although many islands have lakes, the biggest lakes are found on continents. The Caspian Sea is the largest saltwater lake in the world. It lies between eastern Europe and central Asia. Lake Superior is the largest freshwater lake in the world. It is in North America, where half of the world's lakes are found. Minnesota's nickname is the "Land of 10,000 Lakes." It actually has 15,291 lakes, each with an area of 10 acres (4 hectares) or more.

## Groups of lakes

The world map shows that some places have groups of lakes. In North America, five large lakes make up the Great Lakes. In northern Europe, Finland has more than 60,000 lakes across the country. The Great Lakes and the lakes of Finland were made by ice **eroding** massive areas of land.

Another group of lakes lies on the eastern side of Africa. This group includes Lake Victoria, the second-largest freshwater lake in the world. The east African lakes formed in a huge crack in the earth's surface, called the Great Rift Valley, that stretches from Syria in Asia to Mozambique in Africa.

Lake Eyre is the biggest lake on the continent of Australia. It was once part of a huge inland sea. It covers 3,600 square miles (9,300 sqare kilometers). It is also the world's largest temporary lake. When there is very little rain for a few years, the lake disappears completely.

# Lake Landscapes

There are countless different lake shapes, ranging from tiny mountain **tarns** to huge inland seas and from long, thin ribbon lakes to round **crater** lakes. Lake landscapes vary from rolling green hills to bare, rocky **gorges**. Lakes and lake landscapes change all the time. Some changes are natural. Other changes are caused by people.

## Changing landscape

Some lake landscapes change during a single year. This is because they lie in areas where there is a very dry season and a very rainy one, such as Lake Chad in central Africa. Some larger lakes have several different landscapes. The Sea of Galilee, also known as Lake Tiberius, lies in Jordan's Great Rift Valley. This lake is completely surrounded

Morning mists are a common feature of lake landscapes. When the night skies are clear, the moist air above the lake often gets very cold. The water droplets in the cold air turn into mist or fog clouds, which you can see early in the morning. When the sun comes out, the warmed air rises from the lake and the water droplets **evaporate.** Then the mist disappears.

by beaches. However, in the north and northwest, there are flat **plains**, and in the east and southwest, there are cliffs.

Some lakes have sandy shores. Others have banks made of mud. Many lakes have marshland around their edges. This happens where the lake is slowly being filled with fine soil, called **silt**.

## Clear lakes and blue lakes

The water of some lakes, such as the Sea of Galilee, is cool and clear. Other lakes are bright blue. Sometimes this is because the water acts like a mirror and reflects the blue sky. At other times, the blue color is caused by **minerals** in the water, such as in Crater Lake in Oregon.

Crater Lake in Oregon was formed in an **extinct** volcano. When it rains, water runs down the steep sides of the crater and into the **basin**. Water seeps away into the rock. It also **evaporates** into the air when the sun is hot. The moisture becomes **water vapor** and is carried away from the volcano and into the air. Crater Lake is famous for the changing colors of its water, especially its deep blue color.

# How Lakes Are Formed

## The moving earth

Many lakes fill great splits in large masses of rock. These splits, or **faults**, are caused by movement deep down in the crust of the earth. The Rift Valley in eastern Africa is an example of this.

Other lakes have formed in dips made when the surface of the earth crumpled into folds. These folds are made of layers of different types of rock. Lakes occur when a dip is made of a layer of rock that will not soak up the water that runs into it. This kind of rock is known as **impermeable**.

Oxbow or cutoff lakes form gradually as a river carves loops in its channel. The curve of the loop gets rounder while the neck of the loop gets narrower. Then the water of the river flows over the neck, cutting off the loop. In the end, most oxbow lakes become boggy and shrink to nothing.

Lakes are also formed when **landslides** block the ends of valleys. Valleys are carved by the action of streams, rivers, or ice.

## The power of ice

The power of moving ice has formed many of the world's biggest lakes. These lakes were formed by large masses of ice called **glaciers**. Glaciers are pulled down mountains by the force of gravity. As the glaciers slip down the slope, they **scour** out great valleys in the rock. They carry bits of broken rock with them. When the ice finally melts, the rocks get dumped, or deposited, at the ends of valleys. This blocks the valleys, which then fill with water. Lakes formed this way are called glacial lakes. Long, thin glacial lakes are called ribbon lakes. Glaciers higher in mountain ranges scour out smaller dips. They leave a lip of rock at the edge that traps water in the dip. These lakes are called **tarns**.

Many of today's glacial lake **basins** were formed during the last **ice age**. This ice began to retreat about 11,000 years ago, allowing the basins to fill with water.

## Underground lakes

You cannot see all the lakes of the world—some lie underground. These are formed when water seeps through soil and soaks through surface rock until it reaches an impermeable basin. The water cannot soak through the basin, so it sits on top of it. A huge underground lake lies under a large part of Australia.

# The Great Lakes

The five Great Lakes of North America make up the largest body of freshwater in the world. The Great Lakes include Lake Superior, the world's biggest freshwater lake. The other Great Lakes are Ontario, Erie, Huron, and Michigan. They cover a huge area of North America. People have connected the lakes by building **canals.**

## Making and shaping

Many lakes were formed by one action and then reshaped over time by other actions. The Great Lakes are a good example of this. Lake Superior is in what was once a wide valley. To the southeast were low-lying **plains**. Then, in the last **ice age**, huge

The Great Lakes have amazing scenery. Pictured Rocks, on the southeast shore of Lake Superior, are multicolored sandstone cliffs. But the lakes are not just beautiful—they are home to many natural resources. The area around the lakes is rich in **minerals,** such as iron, copper, and silver. Many mines and factories have been built along the lake shores.

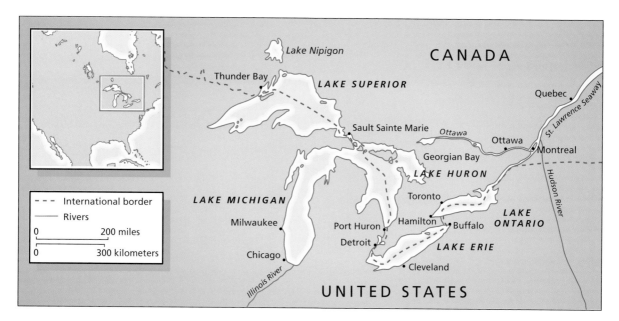

glaciers deepened the valley and gouged large holes in the plains. The valley and plains filled with water and formed the Great Lakes.

Then the lake beds changed again. More than 10,000 years ago, a movement in the earth's crust lifted the northern end of the lakes. This caused the water to drain into the St. Lawrence Seaway.

The Great Lakes are fed by rivers and streams. The amount of water increases with melting snow and ice, called **meltwater**. Lakes higher in elevation feed into the lower lakes through rivers. For example, Lake Superior drains into Lake Huron.

The lakes have huge bays where the lake extends into the land. Some of the lakes have large islands on which people live.

The Great Lakes were made into one of the world's biggest shipping **networks**. Canals were dug between the lakes where the rivers are too shallow or dangerous for boats. In 1959 the St. Lawrence Seaway Project connected the lakes to the Atlantic Ocean with a deep canal. The canal is used by medium-sized ocean-going ships. The lakes are also connected to the Gulf of Mexico through the Illinois Waterway and the Mississippi River. During the cold winters, frozen water can stop all shipping.

# Lake Water

The water levels of lakes rise and fall. Some lakes dry up completely during the hot, dry months of the year. They fill up again during cooler, wetter months. Over many years, lakes can grow or shrink and change their shape. Some turn into marshland, while others turn to dust.

Most lakes are fed by rivers, streams, and melting snow and ice. Some are fed by underground springs. A small amount of lake water comes from raindrops falling on the lake's surface. But however they are fed, lake waters are always on the move.

Lake Erie is one of the Great Lakes of North America. It looks calm in this photograph of Detroit, Michigan. But Lake Erie is quite shallow, which means that in stormy weather, huge swells of water rise from the bottom. This causes large surface waves. Lake Erie can be dangerous for ships, especially in winter when storms are fierce.

## Moving water

Strong winds whip the top layer of water into waves. But lake water also moves beneath the surface. Rivers and streams pour cold water into the warmer top layer of lake water. The cold water sinks because it is heavier than the warm water. The sinking cold water moves the water already there. This is called a **current.** It is like the currents that flow in seas and oceans.

In hot summer months, a lake has a layer of warm water resting on top of a cold layer. In the autumn, the top layer of water cools and sinks. It mixes with the water underneath and causes movement. This disturbs the lake's surface with little choppy waves.

Lake water can also move very slowly around the lake's **basin**, like soup swirling around a bowl. These movements are called **seiches.** Some seiches are caused by strong winds, but most happen because of the earth's rotation.

Lake Chad lies in central Africa. In the wet season the water covers 10,000 square miles (25,900 square kilometers). In the dry season, the lake shrinks to less than half that size. In the northwest, the lake is only about 3 feet (1 meter) deep. In the south it is about 20 feet (6 meters) deep. Lake Chad is getting smaller over time. This is partly because the hotter **climate** is causing more water to **evaporate** into the air. Water is also seeping through the rock in the lake basin.

# Lake Plants

Still or slow-moving freshwater lakes provide a rich habitat for a wide range of plants, from tiny **algae** to large flowering water lilies. Many types of grassy reeds and rushes grow on marshy lake edges. This is known as a **lentic** habitat.

## Leafy lake plants

Most leafy lake plants have waxy leaves and thick stems, which protect them from the water. They also hold their leaves above the water's surface. Some flat leaves float like rafts. The main roots of lake plants reach far down into the **silt** at the bottom of the lake. Sometimes there are very fine, feathery roots called **tendrils** dangling from the stem. These absorb **minerals** from the water around them. The roots of lake plants take in large

Plants and animals that live in the water need oxygen to survive. Lake plants make oxygen when the sun acts on the green cells in their leaves. The *elodea crispa*, found in many parts of the world, is especially good at making oxygen. It has long spiky stems with bright green, thin, curled leaves. Bubbles of oxygen rise from tiny holes in each leaf. *Elodea crispa* is sold for use in ponds and goldfish tanks. The plant provides oxygen for the fish and other animals.

amounts of water. A lot of the moisture **evaporates** through thousands of tiny holes in the plant leaves. Without the holes, the plants would rot.

## Tiny algae

Some freshwater lakes contain very few plants. These lakes often have crystal-clear water right down to the bottom. The edges of the lake are rocky, with no soil in which waterside plants can grow. In the summer, there might be a thin, milky film on the surface of the water. This is made by millions of very tiny plants known as algae that grow when the sun warms the water. Some algae grow even in the coldest water. An orange-pink algae grows in the lakes of Antarctica. Other kinds of algae also grow in saltwater lakes. Some plants have even **adapted** to conditions in the Dead Sea, which is nine times as salty as the ocean.

◇ The white water lily can grow in water up to 10 feet (3 meters) deep. It thrives in many parts of Europe. Its long, strong stems carry large, round, flat leaves, which float on the surface. The cup-shaped flowers also float. The lily's seed pods ripen underwater. When they burst, the seeds float to the surface and are carried far and wide. The very thick bottom of the water lily's stem is called a rhyzome. Long ago, people in northern Europe used it as food.

17

# Animals of the Lakes

In both saltwater and freshwater lakes, animals have **adapted** their bodies and habits to living in and around the water. Lakes are home to many species of reptiles, mammals, amphibians, birds, and fish. But in some crystal-clear freshwater lakes, there are very few animals. There were no fish in Oregon's Crater Lake until 1888, when they were introduced by humans. Some saltwater lakes also have very few animals. Only the brine shrimp has adapted to the salty water of the Dead Sea.

Flamingos flock to Lake Naivasha in east Africa. These birds are well adapted to life on the lakeshore. Their long, curved bills scoop up tiny shellfish, which give them their pink color. Their webbed feet help them stand on soft mud, and long legs keep their feathers above the water. Flamingos nest on mudflats or heaps of mud above the surface of the lake.

# Life in the lake

Many freshwater lake animals are the same as those living in rivers and streams. The Lake Baikal seal in Siberia is the only freshwater seal in the world. Its thick layers of fat help it cope with the freezing waters during the harsh winters.

In hot east and central Africa, the hippopotamus lives along the edges of lakes. During the day it can travel 25 miles (40 kilometers), eating as it goes. Hippopotamuses are good swimmers. They can swim underwater for five minutes. Only their eyes, ears, and nostrils can be seen as they swim.

Amphibians spend part of their lives in the water and part out of it. The adults breathe air, but their **larvae** hatch in the water and breathe through gills. Lakes make good **habitats** for many types of amphibious frogs, toads, and newts.

Freshwater pike fish hide at the shallow edges of large lakes where there are a lot of water plants. Their huge mouths and sharp teeth are adapted for snapping at passing fish. The powan and the vendace are two small fish that live in mountain lakes in northern Europe. They have adapted to swallowing tiny plants and animals called **plankton** that float in the water.

This terrapin, a type of turtle, lives in south and central Europe. It is a reptile, so it breathes air on land, but it often feeds in the water. The terrapin eats fish, amphibians, and sometimes small land animals. It has no teeth, but catches its prey with a horny beak. It likes to live near still waters, so it often chooses lakes. It dives in the water when it is disturbed. A tough shell protects it from other meat-eating animals.

# People of the Lakes

All over the world, people have settled near lakes. For thousands of years, settlers have used lake waters for drinking, cooking, washing, and growing crops. Lakes have provided people with plants and fish to eat. Trees and reeds surrounding the lakes provide material for building homes and boats and for making baskets and mats.

In more recent times, **minerals**, such as iron, copper, and silver, have been mined around lakes. Petroleum oil has also been found. These natural resources provided jobs that attracted many people to the lakes. Ports grew as more farm products, minerals, and manufactured goods were transported across the waters. Towns and large cities rose around these ports.

Chicago is located on low-lying ground next to Lake Michigan. About 170 years ago, Chicago was a tiny lake settlement with only twelve families. Today it is one of the biggest inland ports in the world. The Great Lakes are surrounded by farmland. Chicago began as a trade center for meat and grain, expanding as more industry grew.

# Homes in the lakes

Thousands of years ago, some people made their homes in lakes. This provided protection against enemies and rising lake waters. In quiet lake waters, buildings rested on short wooden stumps called piles. The piles were stuck into mounds of mud or terraces of stone. Stone walls were built around the mud mounds and stone terraces to keep them from falling apart.

Stone Age builders in Wangen, Switzerland, made huge settlements in lakes. Over 50,000 piles were used to hold them up. Later, in the Bronze Age, even bigger settlements were made, with two-story buildings. These ancient people traded leather goods, textiles, and pottery. Today, some communities still build homes in lake water. South Americans build houses in the lakes near the Orinoco and Amazon Rivers.

Lake Michigan has enabled Chicago to become the largest city in the Great Lakes area. This map shows how roads fan out to other towns in the region and how towns stretch along the lake shore.

# A Way of Life—The Luo of Lake Victoria

Lake Victoria lies in east Africa. It is the second-largest freshwater lake in the world. The Luo people began to settle on its eastern shores more than 500 years ago. Before that, they lived further north in Sudan, where they herded cattle on open grassland. But Lake Victoria had everything that they wanted—good pasture for their cattle and lots of fish. They could buy grain grown by the Gusii people on the fertile hillsides nearby. There was also a constant supply of building materials. Many Luo still use the natural lake environment to make a living and to build homes.

This map shows where most Luo settlements lie near Lake Victoria. It also shows the port of Kisumu and the fertile hills around the lake.

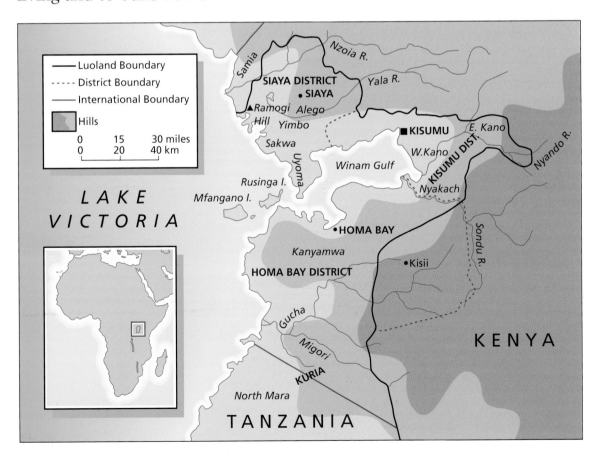

## Making a living

Today, many fishermen still use slender wooden canoes for fishing. They catch mostly long lungfish and tilapia, an African freshwater fish. Traditionally, this fish was preserved by smoking or drying. The Luo fishermen now use modern nets to catch the fish. Some still trap them using long baskets made of dried reeds.

Luo farmers grow crops for export and raise animals. Many people work in transportation, industry, and commerce in the port of Kisumu.

## Building a home

The muddy lake shores provide material for building lakeside homes. Some houses are still built in the traditional way. Wet clay is daubed on a circular framework of poles. The roof is made of poles tied in a cone shape and thatched with stalks of reeds or grain. Clay is used to make pots. Reeds and stalks are woven into baskets.

Large boats carry goods to all parts of Lake Victoria from the port city of Kisumu. Kisumu is also linked to Kenya's coastal port, Mombasa, by a railroad. Nearly a hundred years ago, Kisumu exported animal skins, wild rubber, beeswax, and other natural products. Today, cotton, coffee, and manufactured goods are transported across the water.

# Changing Lakes

## Natural changes

Lakes change all the time. Some lakes get deeper as more ice and snow melt into them. Other lakes get shallower as the water **evaporates** or seeps through the rock below. Over time, some lakes fill up with fine soil, called **silt**. Many lake edges turn into marshland full of reeds and waterweeds. Some lakes end up as wetlands covered in grass and wild flowers. Others are left as **basins** of dry rock.

In recent years, lakes have evaporated more quickly. This is because of general changes in the earth's **climate**. Not everyone agress about what is causing these changes. Some scientists think that the hotter weather is part of a natural temperature cycle. Other scientists think that it is because carbon dioxide and other

The Caspian Sea is the largest lake in the world. Many rivers, including the Volga, flow into it. Over the last few hundred years, many dams have been built on the rivers, and other water is drained to use for **irrigation**. This causes less water to flow into the Caspian Sea. Now, the water evaporates faster than it is replaced. This means that the Caspian Sea is shrinking.

24

gases are building up in the atmosphere around the earth. These gases trap the heat from the sun, causing the earth to become warmer. This is called the greenhouse effect. Scientists believe that humans are causing this build-up of gases by burning fossil fuels, such as oil and coal, and polluting the atmosphere.

Life in the lakes changes as water becomes shallower, more polluted, and there are fewer plants and animals. Natural life is also damaged by polluted rain, called **acid rain**. It kills tiny **algae** that form in lakes during the summer months.

## Man-made changes

In some places, lake water is becoming shallower because rivers are kept from flowing into them. Rivers can be blocked to control flooding or diverted into artificial lakes behind **dams**. The dams provide water to **irrigate** dry farmland. Dams are also built to provide hydroelectric power (HEP) for cities and industry. But when dams are built, people living along the rivers have to move their homes. Natural habitats are destroyed.

◈ When the waters of the Caspian Sea became lower, the land on the lake shores increased. Farmers began to grow crops on it. Factories and a nuclear power station were built. All this activity caused the fishing waters to become more polluted. The dams on the Volga River also kept sturgeon fish from swimming up from the lake to lay their eggs in the river.

# Looking to the Future

Lakes are very useful, busy places. They are beautiful, too. Can nature and people thrive together in and around them? We want a lot from our lakes. We want the animals and plant life to stay as they are. But the beauty of lakes also attracts a lot of tourists to their shores. Tourists have meant more pollution, and many hotels have been built along the lake shores. Both of these destroy the natural beauty.

Lakes are used for transportation, and they provide jobs. Their shores are good places to build factories, which often need water for manufacturing. But many of these factories do not take good care of the lakes. Some use the waters to carry away their

Lake Baikal formed in a split, or rift, in the earth's surface 25 million years ago. It has more than 1,500 of its own species of plants and animals. The lake tells a lot about how life on Earth has changed. This is why it is important to keep the water clean and to preserve the plants and animals in it.

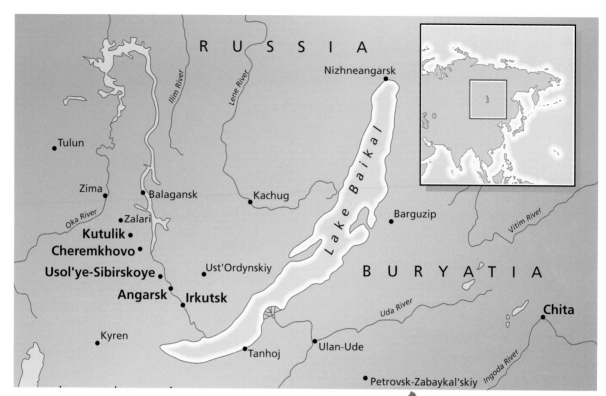

waste. Lakeside forests provide trees that are cut down and floated to sawmills built around the shores. **Minerals** are mined in and around lakes.

## The best of both worlds

The story of Lake Baikal shows how nature and human activity can thrive side by side. Lake Baikal lies in southern Siberia in Russia. It is the world's oldest and deepest lake. In winter and spring, the lake is covered in a thick layer of ice. In the summer and autumn, it is crystal clear. This is because billions of shrimp eat the tiny **algae** and **bacteria** in the water. Lake Baikal's clear waters also made it a good place to make high quality plastics, paper, and cardboard. The factories polluted the waters badly. So in 1987, the factories were forced to find other ways of getting rid of their solid waste. They could no longer pump harmful chemicals into the water. Now the waters are clear again.

The shape of Lake Baikal shows that it has formed in a split in the earth's crust. Many rivers flow into and out of the lake, so any pollution in the lake affects a wider area than just the lake.

# Lake Facts

## The top ten lakes

These are the ten largest lakes in the world. Some of the lakes are called seas. They are really lakes, because they are large bodies of water surrounded by land. The table shows the lakes in order of the area of water they normally hold. But lakes change all the time, so the figure is difficult to calculate, and it changes from time to time.

| | Continent | Area (sq. mi.) | Area (sq km) |
|---|---|---|---|
| Caspian Sea | Asia/Europe | 143,550 | 371,800 |
| Lake Superior | North America | 31,800 | 82,350 |
| Lake Victoria | Africa | 26,000 | 67,350 |
| Lake Huron | North America | 23,010 | 59,600 |
| Lake Michigan | North America | 22,400 | 58,000 |
| Aral Sea | Asia | 15,500 | 40,000 |
| Lake Tanganyika | Africa | 13,000 | 33,750 |
| Lake Baikal | Asia | 12,162 | 31,500 |
| Great Bear Lake | North America | 12,096 | 31,350 |
| Lake Malawi/Nyasa | Africa | 11,430 | 29,600 |

## Highest, lowest, deepest

Highest: Lake Titicaca—12,500 feet (3,811 meters) above sea level.

Lowest: The Dead Sea—1,310 feet (403 meters) below sea level.

Deepest: Lake Baikal—5,315 feet (1,940 meters).

The Aral Sea lies in central Asia. It was once the fourth biggest lake in the world. But its water has been used heavily for **irrigation**. The water level has dropped by more than half in the last 40 years. The water level is now so low that the lake is divided into two.

# Glossary

**acid rain** rainwater that has been polluted by chemicals. Acid rain is caused by gases released into the air from factories and motor vehicles.

**adapt** to change and make suitable for a new use

**algae** simple form of plant life, ranging from a single cell to a huge seaweed

**bacteria** tiny, one-celled organisms, some of which can cause disease

**basin** lake floor shaped like a bowl; or the area of land around a river and the rivers that drain in or out of it

**canal** man-made waterway like a river that is built for boats and ships

**climate** rainfall, temperature, and winds that normally affect a large area

**crater** hole or hollow in the top of a volcano

**current** strong surge of water that flows constantly in the same direction

**dam** wall built across a river valley to hold back water, creating an artificial lake

**erosion** wearing away of rocks and soil by wind, water, ice, or acid

**evaporate** to turn from solid or liquid into vapor, such as water becoming water vapor

**extinct** dead; no longer active

**fault** crack deep in the earth's crust

**flood plain** flat land in a valley bottom that floods regularly

**glacier** thick mass of ice, formed from compressed snow, that flows downhill

**gorge** narrow river valley with very steep sides

**habitat** place where plants and animals live and grow in nature

**ice age** time when snow and ice covered much of the earth

**impermeable** describes a substance that does not allow water to pass through it

**irrigate** supply a place or area with water, for example, to grow crops

**landslide** when the top surface of soil and rock slips down a slope

**larva** (more than one are larvae) undeveloped but active young of animals, such as insects and frogs

**lentic** slow-moving water habitat for animals and plants

**meltwater** water from melted ice and snow

**mineral** substance formed naturally in rocks and earth, such as coal, tin, or salt

**navigable** deep and wide enough for ships to use

**network** system with many connected lines or passages

**plain** area of flat land

**plankton** tiny water plants and animals

**plateau** area of high, flat ground, often lying between mountains

**scour** to rub hard against something, wearing it away

**seiche** slow movement of lake water around its basin

**silt** fine particles of eroded rock and soil that can settle in lakes and rivers, sometimes blocking the movement of water

**tarn** small lake or pool in mountains

**tendril** fine, feathery root

**water cycle** system by which the earth's water is constantly changing from rivers, lakes, and seas to water vapor in the air that falls as rain and drains into rivers, lakes, and seas again

**water vapor** water that has been heated until it forms a gas that is held in the air. Drops of water form again when the vapor is cooled.

# More Books to Read

Armbruster, Ann. *Lake Superior.* Danbury, Conn.: Children's Press, 1996.

Barber, Nicola. *Rivers, Ponds & Lakes.* North Pomfret, Vt.: Evans Brothers, Ltd., 1996.

Miller, Debbie S. *Disappearing Lake: Nature's Magic in Denali National Park.* New York: Walker & Company, 1997.

Morris, Neil. *Lakes.* Austin, Tex.: Raintree Steck-Vaughn, 1997.

Sayre, April P. *Lake & Pond.* Brookfield, Conn.: Twenty-First Century Books, Inc., 1995.

# Index